How to Read Local Archives 1550-1700

F. G. EMMISON
Former County Archivist of Essex

The above is from the heading of a manor court roll of Steeple Bumpstead, 1652

The cover illustration of the 'Secretary Hand' alphabet, from *A Booke Containing Divers Sortes of Hands* (John de Beauchesne and John Baildon, 1571), is reproduced by permission of the Trustees of the British Museum

The Historical Association
59A *Kennington Park Road*, 4JH

1(A) PARISH REGISTER, BOREHAM, 1596

Agnes Martyn wyff of John Martin was buried the viij of Marche
Elizabethe born of a wayfaringe voman was baptized the xth of marche
Clear turner wyff of Tho[mas] turner was buried the xvj of Marche.

Anno D[omi]ni 1596

Wyll[ia]m Crosse son of Thomas crosse was baptized the xxviij of marche
Thomesyn bret daughter of John bret was baptized the xxv of april.
Samuel Clarke and Joan lunt war Maried the xxvj of april.
James Wylie and bridget Annand war Maried the tenthe of May.
Thomas cornwell had two daughters baptized the xxx of May
And war buried the sam weeke.

A fairly clear, average example of Secretary hand except perhaps for the tail to final *n*. In line 2 the first letter of *voman* is merely a slip. The year until 1752 began on 25 March (Lady Day), which explains the heading after 16 March.

Parish registers were instituted in 1538. In 1598 the original paper registers had to be copied on parchment, with the option of copying only from 1558. Most registers, especially those of parishes with a main road, give many entries of vagrants.

1(B) CHURCHWARDENS' ACCOUNTS, CHELMSFORD, 1559

It[e]m payed to them that dyd helpe take downe the Roode – ii^d
It[e] payed to John locker for iij kees for ye Steple dores – viij^d
It[e]m payed to xpofer [Christopher] for wasshyng from mydsomer tell chrystmas – ij^s
It[e]m payed to will[ia]m harrys and his too men for too dayes and a halfe in mendyng the belles – vj^s

Note the normal *h* in *helpe* and the carelessly-written *h* in *them* (line 1); the *h* in *that* is a halfway example. Line 5 shows the special abbreviation for Christopher, also a clear example of *ssh* joined at their tops. The lozenge-shaped sign with a line joining it to a brace was often used. In money entries *s* and *d* are often misread.

The first entry, typical of churchwardens' accounts for 1559, is a reminder that any roods still remaining after the general removal in Edward VI's time and roods re-erected under Mary were pulled down early in Elizabeth's reign.

1(C) HEADING OF CHURCHWARDENS' ACCOUNTS, HORNCHURCH, 1624

Payed by me Phillipp Lenthall Church wardenn Anno p[re]d[icto] for the Rep[ar]ac[i]ons of the churche of Hornechurche: Ornament[es]: vtensill[es]: Comunyon wyne: & other churche necessaries: as followeth

Note the clear contraction very often used for the plural *-es* and the less common extra stroke at the top of *t*. In cursive writing minims, as in *Ornament[es]*, were flattened; but in *Comunyon* the scribe unwittingly helped the modern reader by raising his pen after *u*.

This heading obligingly analyses the main expenses detailed in the actual entries.

1(D) PARISH ACCOUNTS, HORNCHURCH, 1665

	£	s	d
Expences in the time of the plague 1665			
Imprimis to the constable of Southend for watchmen at severall tymes	05	02	06
It[em] paid for two warrants for him	00	02	00
It[em] paid to Talbot for watching at severall times	05	16	00
It[em] to Aldridge for looking to the sick persons at severall tymes	001	10	00

For the notes on plate 1(D) please turn to page 12

Agnes Martyn wyff of John Martin was buried the viij of Marche

Elizabeth borne of a wayfaringe woman was baptized the ix of march

Elner turner wyff of Th. turner was buried the xvj of Marche.

Anno Dñi 1596.

Wyllm Crosse son of Thomas crosse was baptized the xxviij of march

Thomasyn bell daughter of John bell was baptized the xvjth of aprill.

Samuel Clarke and Joan hunt war maried the xvjth of aprill.

James Wylie and bridget Awmond war maried the xviijth of May.

Thomas scutnoll had two daughters baptized ye viij of May And war buried the same weeke.

Item payed to them that dyd helpe take downe the Roode _____ iiij d

Item payed to John lorden for iij dees for ye steeple dores _____ xviij d

Item payed to proses for wasshing from mydsomer till christmas _____ ij s

Item payed to willm harrys and his workmen for toodayes and a halfe in mendyng ye belles _____ xvj d

Copyed by me Nycholas louthall churche warden Anno Dñi for the Regesters off the churche off hornchurche: + ornamente vtensille: communyon wyne: & other thinge necessarie: as ffolloweth

Expences in the tyme of the plague 1665

	£	s	d
Imprimis to the constable of Bowtyme for watchment at severall tymes	05	02	06
It paid for two warrants for gun	00	02	00
It paid to Talbot for watching at severall times	05	16	00
It to Aloridge for looking to the sick persons at severall tymes	001	10	00

Manor of Shenfield. – The View of Frankpledge with the Court of Francis Chauncye Esquire and of Alice his wife there held on 4th Nov. in the 9th year of the reign of our Lady Elizabeth by the grace of God Queen of England, France and Ireland, Defender of the Faith, etc.

This shows a fairly normal heading of a manor court roll in Latin. The double long *s* before *Visus* is a paragraph mark. The dash sign indicating letter(s) omitted, instead of being a separate horizontal stroke, is linked with the last letter to avoid taking up the pen (*Maneriu[m]* and *homagiu[m]*). The superscript hook sign for *er* or *ar*, as in *Armig[er]i*, is also used for *or* in *vx[or]is*, both in line 1. Plate 10 gives a somewhat longer beginning of a manor court record in English.

Of the two kinds of manor court, the Court Baron with View of Frankpledge (above) was the lord's court, to which the tenants owed suit (attendance). Essoins were excuses for non-attendance. It dealt chiefly with registration of changes in tenure of copyholds through death or sale. The Court Leet (plate 10) was a petty court for trial of offences by the homage (jury composed of the freeholders and tenants).

Italics were often used to distinguish a heading or important phrase. Some words such as 'sacramentum' had their special abbreviations.

The lord of every manor, or the inhabitants, was responsible for providing and maintaining archery butts, pillory, stocks, cucking-stool, whipping-post, pound, and standard weights and measures. Want = lack.

Most manor court rolls (A, B above) are formal records in which the lord's steward used standard phraseology (and mainly in Latin until 1733 except during 1653–60). Presentments in the actual language of the foreman of the homage or manorial jury are rarer and much more difficult to read if he was not used to writing (or spelling), but it is rewarding to meet the challenge as they are more interesting. In line 2 the added phrase (in Latin) is in the hand of the court steward.

By an Act of 1570 caps were to be worn by all males above the age of 7 on Sundays and holy days to help the woollen industry. For bows, see 5(B).

2(A) BEGINNING OF MANOR COURT ROLL, SHENFIELD, 1567

Maneriu[m]) Visus Franc[i] pleg[ii] cum Curia Francisci
de Shenffeylde) Chauncye Armig[er]i et Alicie vx[or]is sue
Ib[ide]m tent[a] Quart[o] die Novembris Anno
regni D[omi]ne n[ost]re Elizabeth[e] dei gra[ti]a
Anglie Francie et Hib[er]nie Regine fidei
defensoris &c [etcetera] nono,

Esson[ia] [Essoins] Johanna [Joan] Strete vid[ua] [widow]
Homagiu[m] [The Homage] Joh[ann]es [John] Exytor,
Will[elm]us Elyment, Thom[a]s Symond, Thom[a]s Reynold[es],
Will[elm]us Fuller, Will[elm]us Newman, Joh[ann]es Symond,
Georgius Manfeld, Will[elm]us Wharton, Joh[ann]es Fuller,
Xpoferus [Christopher] Smyth, Joh[ann]es Notte, jur[ati] [sworn].

2(B) EXTRACT FROM MANOR COURT ROLL, AVELEY, 1624

Nunc de Leta [now concerning the Leet (court)]
Juratores p[re]d[icti] dicunt sup[er] sacr[ament]u[m] suu[m] et vlterius p[re]sentant provt sequitur in his Anglicanis verbis sequentibus vizt [videlicet]. [The aforesaid jurors say upon their oath and further present as follows in these English words following, namely]
Imp[r]imis we p[re]sent that we want a Common pounde, a bushell a pecke, a cookeing stole, and a whipinge post and that the Pillory is out of repaire
Item we p[re]sent that the Cookinge stoole pond wanteth scoureinge.

2(C) ORIGINAL PRESENTMENTS OF MANORIAL JURY, TAKELEY, 1587

It[e]m we fynde furthe [for the] lete nycolas eynggegolde to [be] ovre [our] constabel. Juratus est modo [he is now sworn]
It[e]m we fynde ovre selfes In Defate [default] for note waryng ovre capes & not eusyng [using] ovre bowes.

Maneriu[m] ...

Johannes Strelebull

Willelmus ...

Willelmus Fullour

Nunc de ...

Note the two forms of initial long *s* (one being similar to initial *h*), also the various forms of medial *h* and the conjoined *sh* in *shalbe* (a normal spelling).

Vestry books relate mainly to poor relief (detailed minutes before 1660 are unfortunately not common), and both extracts illustrate the way in which every parish, under the settlement laws, tried to save expense by removing paupers or potential paupers, as well as vagrants, to another parish. Account-books of overseers of the poor (common) and constables (rare) record in detail the cost of relieving poverty and of dealing with vagrancy.

The general slant gives the impression that it is all italic, but it is in fact a cursive Secretary hand except for italic *e*, *l*, *b* and several capitals. The interlocked heads of *ff* and long *ss* (joined on to final *e*) of *Francisse* make it difficult to read.

Vestry meetings, after formal opening in the church vestry, usually adjourned to the inn (or to a different inn at each meeting in turn, if there were several in the parish); but in Finchingfield the strongly Puritan parishioners met at each manorhouse or farmhouse in rotation. Under an Act of 1589 anyone keeping an 'inmate' who might later need relief was fined by the manor court or indicted at Quarter Sessions; the last paragraph (*not illustrated*) records an even harsher decision by this vestry.

3(A) VESTRY MINUTES, BRAINTREE, 1619

Imprimis it is agreed that Arbinger being sent by his father backe againe after that by the Justices warrant he was sent from Brainctre to him shalbe corrected as a vagrant and be sent w[i]th a pasporte backe againe to Stebbing to his father
Memorand[um] at this meeting the widdow Wilsons sonne was delivered to George Billingale to be bound w[i]th him as his apprentice according as it was agreed the last meeting
It is agreed that Robert Eliott being growne aged and poore shalbe put into the Almeshouse wherin Baldwin is and he turned out

3(B) VESTRY MINUTES, FINCHINGFIELD, 1626

At the meeting at Mr Kemps at Spaines Hall October 23 1626
I[mpri]mis, It is agreed that [non]e of us shall relieve any roague or vagabond but shall bring them to the constable to have them punished
Item It is agreed that John Choate & Henry Taylour shall talk with goodman How about security to the towne to discharg the towne of Francisse Benson, or if he will not then they to deale with Nathaniell Waite about removing him
Item for the preventing of more charge of poore no man shall let a cottage to any of an other towne, or to new married couples who were not borne in the towne and if any man shall refuse to agree to this order, his cottage shall be indited if it be within compasse of the statute vnlesse they will consent to let it to the overseirs, or put none into it, without there approbation[n]

Imprimis it is agreed that disbinger being (but by the Justice
warrant against after that by the Justice warrant was
but from Branden to him shalbe referred as a vagrant
and be sent not a vagrant borne againe to Stebbing to be
kept

Item it is agreed at his meeting the neighbors some was
delivered to George Bishop also to be bound not him as
his apprentice entering my as it was againe by himself some
It is agreed that Robert Eliott being removed againe into Baldwin
poore shalbe sent into the the poore in to or shall out

At the meeting of the Company at Spaniss Hart ofober
23 1626

Imprimis it is agreed that ... of us shall ... and rogues or vagabonds
... being done to be trusted

Item it is agreed that for ... good men have about ...
... to shall

4(A) PRESENTMENT AT COURT OF QUARTER SESSIONS, 1562

It[e]m they [*written above* we *struck through*] p[re]sent also for oure Sou[er]aygn lady the Quene that on mydlent sonday last past there was a foteball play at the sayde Annys [i.e. Agnes *written above* alys *struck through*] Grene wydow the p[ar]lysshe of Stonedon agaynst the p[ar]lysshe of Keldon and play at the cardys all the nyght also co[n]trary to the Statute [*written above* Staty *struck through*] in that case p[ro]vydyd.

4(B) EXTRACT FROM ORDER BOOK OF QUARTER SESSIONS, 1651

Vpon the humble Petic[i]on of John Stotter settinge forth that servinge in the Trayned Band[es] in the Regim^t of Coll[onel] Mathews, in the late expedic[i]on to worcester, he received an hurte in his body whereof he hath ever since layne sicke, & disabled thereby to p[ro]vide for himselfe and family, And prayinge some releife, It is ordered that the Tr[easur]er for the west division doe pay vnto him the sum[m]e of Forty shilling[es], for supply of his wants in this his greate necessity.

The writer uses an *a* from a hand of earlier date than that of Secretary. Note the flourish above *p* (for *pro*) in the third word, the stroke through the stem of *p* written without taking the pen up (for *per*) in line 3 (twice), and the stroke in the last word brought forward through the stem of *p* (for *pro*); the normal contraction for *pro* was written as below, line 6.

The crimes and offences dealt with at County and Borough Quarter Sessions were mostly recorded in the formal indictments (in Latin). Many of these were drawn up from the actual presentments made by the Grand or Petty Juries, written in English by the foreman of the jury in his own language. Agnes Grene's alehouse was the scene of the offences. The lower ranks were prohibited from playing various games which tempted them away from archery practice or into gambling.

The first word is in italic; *h*, *b*, initial *s*, *C* and *M*, also in italic, show how Secretary was gradually superseded. But, unlike this 'mixed' hand, most MSS. of c.1650–1700 were written wholly in one or other script. By an Act of 1601 J.P.s levied a rate for relief of wounded soldiers.

5(A) EXTRACT FROM BOROUGH CUSTOMS BOOK, MALDON, 1609

Line 1 shows the scribe's indulgence in a few decorative letters. There are seven-minim and six-minim words in line 2.

Market trading was usually restricted to the period between the ringing of the opening and closing bells. This is No. 80 of the 92 customs and by-laws. The range of subjects covered by Borough Court records is even wider than that of County Quarter Sessions records. This Maldon miscellany omits reference to its maritime affairs.

Also the Market bell shalbe Rounge at one of the clock in ye
After none both in winter and sommer and that all menne shall
leave sellinge of such victuals & corne as they have to sell at the
same houre vppon paine of forfetinge the same corne and vittels
except butchers dwellinge in the same towne [line filled up with
squiggles]

5(B) EXTRACT FROM BOROUGH RECORD BOOK, MALDON, 1573

A beautiful example of Secretary hand written by a professional scrivener. As *furnished* (i.e. fully equipped) is a common word in this MS. the scribe abbreviated it.

By an Act passed in Mary's last year (1558), every adult male was obliged to provide himself with specified armour or weapons related to his position, and from 1569 onwards the Spanish threat led to the Act being reinforced. All these items of Eliizabethan armour will be found in the *Shorter Oxford Dictionary*.

Armour

W. twedie gen[erosus] [gentleman]	– viijli	one coate of plate fur[nished], one blacke bill or halbert, one longe bowe, one shefe of arrowes, and one stele cappe or scull
Tho[mas] Well[es]	– vli	vt sup[r]a [as above]
W. Vernon gen[erosus]	– xli	one almaine ryvette, coate of plate or brigandine furnished, one haquebutt, one murrian or sallet, and one longe bowe, and one shefe of arrowes, one stele cappe or scull.

5(C) EXTRACT FROM BOROUGH SESSIONS BOOK, MALDON, 1609

Note how long *s* and *f* are written in two strokes – the first, downward, bold and tapering; the second, an upper loop, sometimes not joined to the first but joined to the next letter, especially in *sh-*, *st-*, *so*, *ft-*. The extra top stroke of *a* is not uncommon.

The extracts show two of the six clauses in the recognisance or bond of an alehouse-keeper applying for a licence. No. 2 (not illustrated) reads: 'He shall not permit or suffer any playinge at the cardes, dice, tables [backgammon], quoytes, loggattes [little logs thrown at stakes (see *Hamlet*, V, i)], bowls, or any other unlawful game.'

3. It[e]m that he shall not harbour in his said howse barnes stables, or other where any Rogues, Vagabond[es] sturdye beggers, masterles men, or other suspected p[er]son or p[er]sons whatsoever

4. It[e]m that he shall nether sell nor vtter any Beere Ale or other victuall vppon the Sabothe daie or holydaye during the tyme of dyvine service or sermon, be it in the forenone or afternone

Armour

one coate of plate fine, one blacke bill or halbert, one longe bowe,
one sheffe of arrowes, and one steele cappe or skull

one almaine ryvett, coate of plate or brigandine furnisht, one
sagnebutt, one murrian or stele cap, one longe bowe, and one

6 WILL OF A RADWINTER FARMER, 1567

In the name of god amen 30 of Aprill 1567 I Will[ia]m norfolke of radwinter et c[etera]
Doe make this my testam[en]t et c first I co[m]mitt my Soule to allmightie god et c
It[e]m I geve to John my Sonne & helaine my Daughter iiij^{li} a pec[e] to m[ar]garet my
daught[er] iiij^{li} vj^s viij^d to Jone my daught[er] xx^s So y^t [that] the iiij^{li} w[hi]ch I have
geven to heleine my Daughter shall remaine in the hand[es] of the church wardons & that
w[hi]ch I Doe allowe vnto John yf he vse not his sist[er] heleine well & suffer her to have
chamber rowme quietlie Shall remaine vnto the vse of heleine & be kepte as the other
before in the hand[es] of the churchwardons to be d[elivered] to her as they shall see mete
and convenie[n]t, It[e]m I geve to helene my wife her fether bed y^t she brought me her
materas j paier of ye best Shetes & one paier of blankett[es] allso to the pore iij^s iiij^d. to be
p[ai]d by ye churchwardens as they Shall thinke mete. Allso I geve to W^m my sonne
x^{li} whome I make my exec[utor] to gether w[ith] his sister M[ar]garet & Thom[a]s
Sparkes my ouersear w[hi]ch Thom[a]s Shall have for his paines takinge xx^s at the selling
of my good[es] ye rest of my good[es] remayning & unbequethed my dett[es] p[ai]d I geve
to W^m my Sonne to his owne vse for eu[er] more p[ro]vided allwaies that after the dethe
of helene my Daught[er] ye howse called Jevdes shall Remaine to W^m my Sonne & yf
he die with oute yssue it Shall remaine to my Sonne John & his heires for euer Witnes
Wm Harrisonn John Flacke & others.

In rapidly written secretary hand the *e* tended to be carelessly formed, as in *Shetes* and *paier*
(line 15), *mete* and *geve* (17), and especially *whome* (18) and *helene* (13, 24). The scribe enjoyed
writing his long-tailed *g*. *Jeudes* (now Judes Farm) ends with a meaningless squiggle. Note the
double *ff* in the last line, the variant forms of the *er* (or *ar*) sign, the *pro* contraction (23), and trace
the penstrokes in y^e and y^t. The special abbreviation *D'* (12) is not uncommon.

The first witness is the author of the remarkable contemporary social history, the *Description of
England*, which appeared in Holinshed's *Chronicles* (1577–87), much used by Shakespeare and other
dramatists. Harrison was Rector of Radwinter and probably drew up this will for the farmer (the
Essex Assizes records reveal that four pigs had been stolen from the testator in 1559). In two
well-known passages Harrison commented on the then recent improvements in beds and bedding
amongst country folk (featherbeds in place of straw pallets) and in tableware (pewter in place of
'treene', i.e. wooden, platters): see next illustration.

Expressed briefly, wills of most substantial people were proved in the Prerogative Courts of
Canterbury and York (for the southern and northern parts of the country respectively) and are now
in the Public Record Office and York Institute of Historical Research. Nearly all other wills are
in local (mostly county) record offices. The majority exist both as originals and registered copies.
The former bear the signatures (or marks) of the testators and witnesses; the latter are usually easier
to read. During our period overseers as well as executors were usually appointed.

Notes relating to plate 1(D).

A late example of pure Secretary handwriting invaded by no italic letters. Note the long (but not
unusual) separate upper stroke of *d* and the final flourishes of *x*, *g* and *h*. The extra *O* in the last
line is a clerical slip. The modern £ sign represents the first letter of *Libri* with the contraction mark
through it.

Hornchurch was divided into two wards, North End and South End, for each of which separate
overseers of the poor and constables were appointed. The spread of the Great Plague of London
can be traced and dated in many surviving registers and parish accounts.

In the name of god amen 30 of Aprill 1567 I [Martin]
[Norfolk] of [Wadswinter] etc do make this my testament
etc [First] I comitt my soule to allmightie god etc
etc [Item] I geve to John my sonne & Helene my
daughter mt a pot to Margaret my daughter vjs viijd
to [Jone] my daughter vjd. [also] the mt vjd I have
geven to Helene my daughter shall remaine in the
handes of the church wardens & that vjd I do allowe
unto John yf he will not his [sister] Helene well & suffer
her to have chamber roome ynethe [she] shall remaine
unto the rest of Helene & to kept at the [after] lenton
in the handes of the churchwardens to be [done] to [prai]
they shall see mete and [convenient] & so I geve to Helene
my neife her [defered] & she brought me for matesal
1 paier of the best shetes & one paier of blankett also to
the pore my [deere] to be pd by the churchwardens as they
shall thinke mete — also I geve to [John] my sonne
etc whome I make my exector to gether to his [sister]
Margaret & Thomas Sparke my [overseer] [both] them
shall have for his [paines] takinge vjd at the [billing]
of my goodes & rest of my good remayninge & [unbequethed]
my dettes pd. I geve to John my sonne to the more
[rest] for [our more] provided allwaies that after the [sell]
of Helene my daughter & house called [Jendes] shall
remaine to John my sonne etc yf he die without
[issue] it shall remaine to my sonne John etc his
heires for ever [witnes] Mr garrisone John
[Clarke] etc others ———

7(A) EXTRACT FROM WILL OF A BRADWELL HUSBANDMAN, 1580

. . . ITem I give vnto Johane Dale my dawghter one fetherbedd complete with the posted bedsted with the white sealinge ITem I give vnto her iij pewter platters and iij pewter disshes & a kettle of a gallon and a half All whiche legacies I will shalbe given and delivered vnto her at the daye of her mariage or at the age of xxiiij^tie yeres which of them shall first happen. ITem I give vnto John Medcalf of Bradwell aforesayde my blacke fustian doblett and my blacke freise Jerkyn

The writer shows the difference between *f* and long *s* very clearly. His conjoined *st*, *sh* and *ssh* are also easy to read. In line 7 the figure would be spoken as 'four and twentie', hence the final *-tie*. Fustian and frieze were coarse cloths made of cotton and flax (fustian) and wool (frieze).

7(B) EXTRACT FROM WILL OF A BURNHAM MARINER, 1580

. . . ITem I will and bequeathe to Wenifreth my wief my p[ar]te half of my hoyd called repentaunce w[i]^th the half of all thing[es] belonginge to the foresaid hoie, ITem I bequeathe my koke called the wenne to my foresaide wief w[i]^th all thing[es] belonginge

Written by the same scribe as (A), but more sloping, perhaps through a differently cut quill.
A hoy was a small vessel, rigged like a sloop. A cock, or cockboat, was a dinghy. Half or quarter shares of such craft often appear in wills.

7(C) EXTRACT FROM WILL OF A WIVENHOE SEAFARINGMAN'S WIFE, 1694

. . . Item I give and bequeath unto my Said loveing husband Oone Boat or Skiff w[hi]^ch I lately bought of John Peck of Wivenhoe Boatbuilder w[i]^th all the app[urtenances] w[ha]^tsoever to the said Boat or Skiff belonging to him & his heires for ev[er] p[re]sently aft[er] my de[cea]se

Written near the end of the 17th century, this is an example of Secretary hand, then almost obsolete, still being used by a professional writer, though several characters betray italic influence. After 1700 it is rare to find the signs for *pre* and *er*, but lawyers' clerks continued to abbreviate words like *appurtenances* until very recently.
Wills throw light on many aspects of religious, social and economic life, especially on clothes, plate, jewellery, household furniture, kitchen utensils and tradesmen's and craftmen's equipment and tools.

tenure yarde of Bradwell aforesayde / Item I give unto
Johane Dale my daughter one fetherbedd complete with
the posted bedsted withe the white balinge Item I give
unto her iij pewter platters and iij pewter disshes &
a bottle of a gallon and a halfe All whiche legandes I will
shalbe given and delivered unto her at the daye of her
mariage or at the age of xxiiij. yeres whiche of them
shall furst happen / Item I give unto John Medralfe
of Bradwell aforesayde my blacke fustian doblett and
my blacke friste Jerkyn / Item I give unto william

of Burnham, Item I will and bequeathe to
Wenifrede my witt my pte halfe of my horde called
repentaunce with the halfe of all thinges belonginge unto
the foresaide hoie, Item I bequeathe my hoie called
the Renne to my foresaide witt with all thinges belonginge

my Executors after nominated Item I give and bequeathe unto
my said loving husband oone Boat or Skiffe which I lately bought
of John Perk of Rivenhoe Boatbuilder with all thinges whatsoever to
the said Boat or Skiff belonging to him his heirs for ever Item hastingdorf

A true and p[er]fecte Inventarye of All and singuler the good[es] and Chattells of Thomas Eve of Goodeaster late Deceased made and taken the 9th Daye of Aprill 1618 prised bye Thomas Lucken of the p[ar]ishe of Mashburye gent[leman] Rob[er]t Sorrell of the same and Francis Marshall of the p[ar]ishe of Goodeaster yeomen

Imprimus in the hall one table withe a frame one bible withe Certayne other bookes and some Small Implementes of househould stuffe prized att – xxx^s

Item in the p[ar]lor one Joyned bedstead withe one fetherbed furnished one Cupboard and three Chestes withe other Implementes there prised att – v^li vj^s viij^d

Item in the Chamber ou[er] the p[ar]lor two boarded bedsteades and two flockbed[es] furnished two Chestes withe other Implementes there priseid att – iij^li iij^s iiij^d

Item in the Chamber ou[er] the hall Certayne wheate two hogges of bacon some small Cheeses withe other trifles there prised att – iiij^li ij^s

Item in the butterye two hoggesheades three small barrells withe Certayne brasse and pewter there prised att – ij^li x^s vj^d

Apart from two words in lines 2 and 15 the plural *-es* is always written in full; *barrells* (line 21) shows the modern form of plural. The first word in line 8 is a misspelling for Latin *imprimis* (first). Note the ways in which *ff, fl, sh, ss* and *st* are joined at their tops.

The rest of the inventory deals with the kitchen, the 'boultinghouse' (outhouse for bolting, i.e. sifting the bran or coarse grain), the milkhouse, the malthouse and the chamber over it, the barn, the testator's linen and 'wearing apparel', and the standing corn. It is clear that he was a yeoman.

Inventories had to be prepared and the deceased testator's goods 'prised', i.e. appraised or valued, by neighbours for purpose of probate of the will. Many thousands of inventories have survived, but while some local record offices have an almost complete series, in others there are very few.

A true and pfecte Inventorye of All and singuler
the goode and chattells of Thomas Eve of [Coderston]
late deceassed made and taken the [9]th daye of
Aprill 1618 praised by Thomas [Turton] of the
[gishe] of [Musbarye] yent Robt [Sauer ...]
[some] and Francis Marshall of the gishe of
[Coderston] yeomen

Imprimis in the hall one tabb with a frame
one bibb with dortoyne other [bookes] and some
small Implements of housgould stuffe praised at } vee[?]

Item in the [gler] one [Joyned] bedsted with
one [flockbed] furnished one cupboard and three } [o xij praised]
chestes with other Implements there praised at —

Item in the Chamber ad the [gler] two boarded —
bedstades and two [flockbode] furnished two chestes } [iij iiij vij]
with other Implements there praised at ————

Item in the Chamber ad the hall dortoyne [vessel]
two goyges of baron some small Chestes with other } [vij ij b]
[vtensilles] there praised at ————

Item in the buttorye two [goygesheades] there small
barrelles with dortoyne brass and powter there } [ij vj ij]
praised at ————

9. DEED OF GIFT BY A STEEPLE BUMPSTEAD GENTLEMAN, 1585

OM[N]IBUS CHRISTI fidelibus ad quos hoc presens scriptum p[er]ven[er]it Ric[ard]us Fitche de Bumpsted ad Turrim in com-[itat]u Essex[ie] Gentleman SAL[UT]E]M in d[omi]no sempiter-nam SCIATIS me prefatu[m] Ric[ard]um Fitche pro diversis bonis causis et considerac[i]o[n]ibus me ad hoc movent[ibus] DEDISSE Concessisse feoffasse libe[r]asse et hoc presenti script[o] meo confirmasse Thome Fitche de Cavendishe in Com[itatu] Suff[olkie] filio et heredi apparenti mei pred[i]c[t]i Ric[ard]i Fitche et hered[ibus] suis OM[N]IA et sing[u]la illa mesuagia gardina Orta horta domus edificia terras ten[emen]ta prata pascua pastur[a] bosc[os] subbosc[os] et hereditament[a] mea quecunq[ue] scituat[a] iac[entia] et existent[ia] in p[ar]ochia et campis de Bumpsted ad Turrim p[re]d[icto] aut alubi in d[i]c[t]o com[itatu] Essex[ie] modo in tenura spossessione sive occupac[i]one mei pred[i]c[t]i Ric[ard]i Fitche aut assign[orum] meorum (EXCEPT[IS] tamen et Reservat[is] michi prefat[o] Ric[ard]o Fitche et hered[ibus] meis vno Ten[emen]t[o] cu[m] gardino voc[ato] Hostelers et tribus croftis sive cl[a]usis terre quoru[m] primum voc[atum] Hostelers croft s[e]c[un]d[u]m voc[atum] Dunnigates et terciu[m] voc[atum] Parke crof[es] in Bumpsted p[re]d[icto]) H[AB]ENDUM tenendu[m] et gaudendu[m] Om[n]ia et sing[u]la pred[icta] Mes[uagia] gardina Orta horta domus edificia terr[as] ten[emen]ta hereditamenta et cetera premissa cu[m] suis p[er]tin[enciis] vniu[er]sis (except[is] preexcept[is]]) prefat[o] Thome Fitche hered[ibus] et assign[atis] suis ad solum opus tamen et vsum mei prefati Ric[ard]i Fitche durante tot[o] termi[n]o vite mei pred[i]c[t]i Ric[ard]i Fitche absq[ue] Impetic[i]one alicuius vasti et post decessum mei pred[i]c[t]i Ric[ard]i tunc ad opus et vsum pred[icti] Thome Fitche hered[um] et Ass[ignatorum] suorum Imp[er]p[etuu]m de Capit[a]libus d[omi]nis feod[i] illius p[er] servicia inde debita et de iure consuet[a] ET EGO vero pred[ictus] Ric[ard]us Fytche et hered[es] mei Om[n]ia et sing[u]la suprad[i]c[t]a ten[emen]ta et Cetera premissa cu[m] p[er]tin[enciis] suis vniu[er]sis prefat[o] Thome Fitche hered[ibus] et Ass[ignatis] suis ad vsus et Intenc[i]o[n]es pred[icta] contra me hered[es] et Ass[ignatos] meos warrant[izabimus] et Imperp[etuu]m defendem[us] p[er] present[es] IN cuius Rei testimoniu[m] huic presenti script[o] meo sigillum meum apposui dat[um] decimo sept[imo] die mensis Septembris Anno Regni d[omi]ne n[ost]re Elizabethe die gr[ati]a Angl[ie] Frauncie et hib[e]rnie R[egi]ne fidei defensoris &c vicesimo Septimo 1585.

p[er] me Ric[ardu]m Fytche

Condensed translation of plate 9

To all the faithful of Christ to whom this present writing shall come Richard Fitche of Steeple Bumpsted . . . greeting in the Lord everlasting. Know ye that I . . . for divers good causes . . . have given granted enfeoffed delivered and by this my present writing confirmed to T.F. . . . all and singular those messuages gardens yards orchards outhouses buildings lands tenements meadows feedings pastures woods under-woods and hereditaments whatsoever . . . in . . . S.B. . . . now in my tenure . . . (excepting . . . one tenement with a garden called Hostelers . . .) to have hold and enjoy all [as above] . . . to T.F. . . . to my sole behoof and use however . . . during the whole term of my life . . . without impeachment of any waste and after my death . . . to . . . T.F. . . . of the chief lords of that fee by the services therefor owed and of right accustomed. [Warranty clause.] In witness whereof I have set my seal to this present writing dated 17th Sept, 20th year of Eliz, 1585.

A fine piece of penmanship using regular Secretary. The initial *O* is a simple example of decorative 'strapwork'. The writer made full use of (1) suspension (omission of end of word), e.g. line 2, *comitatu*, and (2) contraction (either by a horizontal dash or by a flourish always above the omitted letter(s)). The special sign for *er* is used twice in *vniuersis* and in line 1, *peruenerit* without lifting the pen. In lines 7 and 14 the medieval contraction for *-que* is seen. In line 8 *alubi* and *spossessione* are clerical slips rather than bad Latin!

Cressing A Court Leet and Court Baron 17th of Aprill 1654. W.L. Gent Stwd

William Witham Gent

Homage: Francis ffrench, John Stokes, Saml Woodward, Piter Rust | John Draper, Henry Ardley, John Woodward, Saml Woodward | Saml Dynes, John Warner, John Godfrey, Edwd Marsh } sworne

De faltrs of the decenars amced at 4d each

They present Wm Yellop for not scouring a ditch cont in length 15 rods lying in Polcats lane to be done by ye first of Augt on pain of 5s.

Ralph Green to lay a wholve for passag: into the Groves by first of Augt on pain of 5s.

Edwd Marsh to scour a ditch called Gulls 20 rodds by ye same time on pain of 20d.

Wm Witham to lay a wholve over the end of Groves lane on pain of 5s.

John Warner to Scour next the highway going to a peece of land called Groves into the lands of one Poley by Michmas on pain of 5s.

ffrancis ffrench hath letten a cott without 4 acres of land to it according to the statute wherefore he hath forfited to the Lord 10s.

Tho. Huntsman dig'd a pitt cont in length 3 feet in highway agst a place called Binnets to be filld up by Midsumer on pain of 5s.

10 MANOR COURT BOOK, CRESSING, 1654

CRESSING   A COURT Leet and Court Baron 17th of Aprill 1654. W.L.   Gent[leman] St[ewar]d

William Witham Gent.

Homage	Francis French	John Draper	Saml Dynes	
	John Stokes	Henry Ardley	John Warner	sworne
	Sam[ue]l Woodward	John Woodward	John Godfrey	
	Peter Rust	Saml Woodward	Edwd Marsh	

Defalters of the decenars am[er]ced at 4d each

They p[re]sent Wm Yellop for not scouring a ditch cont[aining] in length 15 rods lying in Polcats lane to be done by ye first of Augt on pain of 5s.

Ralph Green to lay a wholve for passage into the Groves by first of Augt on pain of 5s.

Edwd Marsh to scour a ditch called Gulls 20 rodds by ye same time on pain of 20d.

Wm Witham to lay a wholve over the end of Groves lane on pain of 5s.

John Warner to Scour next the highway going to a p[ar]cell of land called Groves into the lands of one Poley by Mich[ael]mas on pain of 5s.

Francis French hath letten a cott[age] w[i]thout 4 acres of land to it according to the statute wherefore he hath forfeited to the Lord 10s.

Tho. Huntsman dig'd a pitt cont. in length 3 feet in highway ag[ain]st a place called Bennets. to be filld up by Midsum[m]er on pain of 5s.

For the notes please see opposite